KISS
of
DEATH
DITTIES

Book by BEKA

Art by Valerie Fachman
(a.k.a. Valenka)

Acknowledgements

Thanks for professional services go to Marta Nicholas and Archie Terrance.

<u>My utmost appreciation for all support and contributions is given to</u>:

Cynthia, Mary, Kari, Monique, John, Nadine, Yolanda, D.W., Steve & Carol, Donna, Barry, Lizzie, Sandra, Carol-Ann, Jan, Chelle, Phebe, Lee, Herb & Judy, Dan, Johanne, Claire, Sandi, Christine E., Christine K., Adria and most especially to my artist and friend, Val, and last, but definitely not least —Meemoo.

FOREWORD

By John Borowski, filmmaker/author

I first met Beka when I was producing my first film, *H.H. Holmes: America's First Serial Killer*. She auditioned for the Voice-over role of a grieving widow whose husband and children were murdered by the serial killer Holmes. I asked actresses to call my answering machine and cry. I selected Beka for the role from all of the auditions left on my answering machine as hers was the most convincing. Beka and I have been inseparable since. Beka has many talents. In addition to being an amazing actress, singer, and photographer, she is also a great writer. Having a dark sense of humor myself, when I read *Kiss of Death Ditties*, I immediately fell in love with the material. Many artists translate their feelings into art and I am glad that Beka did the same! My motto is: "Study a serial killer, not become one!" I have also enjoyed the femme fatale character, the devious dames featured in many classic noir movies and novels who lure men to their demise by seducing them with their beauty. I laughed out loud at many of the ditties and I hope that you, the reader, enjoy this book as much as I do. I call Beka my scream queen because we have worked on numerous short films where I make sure that Beka has a great scream scene in the film. She has let out many screams in this gem of a book – that it is no wonder I find it a perfect complement to my Serial Killer Documentary/Book Genre and hope my followers get a kick out of it too! I truly hope there is a sequel to *Kiss of Death Ditties* and I look forward to working on future projects with Beka for as long as possible. Beka's talent is unsurpassed. I wonder….would she find a way to kill ME off in the sequel????

With him I was always Blue,
Till I shot him— in the loo!

Yellow roses, Yellow brick road;
Too bad that he turned into a toad.
Even though all that glittered was Gold,
Love turned to dust
So kill him I <u>must:</u>
After one swift blow—he's dead cold!

He always made me feel *hot*, and in the Pink,
Till his philandering drove me to this brink:
I washed his hair lovingly with ink,
Then drowned him— in the kitchen sink!

He was a cheeky Silver-tongued devil;
In this affair I saw no Silver lining.
So I lacquered him to death— in sleep— in Silver!
(*HOW EVIL!*)
{And no, I won't be pining.}

He always made me see Red,
Till I shot him dead—in bed!

Like a gloss he set me all a-shimmer
and Bronzed my heart,
Then said we must part.
Now he's as heavy as lead
At the ocean bottom—dead!

He loved his car better than me by far;
Any little taint, he'd fall in a faint.
Old parts that would mar, he'd keep in a jar.
His feelings for me were *far* under par and feint.
Daily the car was always the star!
I wanted to pour over it buckets of paint.
(After all, a Saint—*no way*—I ain't!)
I decided worse by far would be TAR!
Told the story of the sight in a bar,
How we all laughed: Har, Har!! Har, Har!!

At first he is the Cat's MEOW;
Oh, he makes you purr and _how_ !
Then claws come out, and how you ROW.
Fur goes flying... OW! *OW*!! *OW!!!*
You have to end this soon somehow:
So you sic on him a big BOW-WOW!!

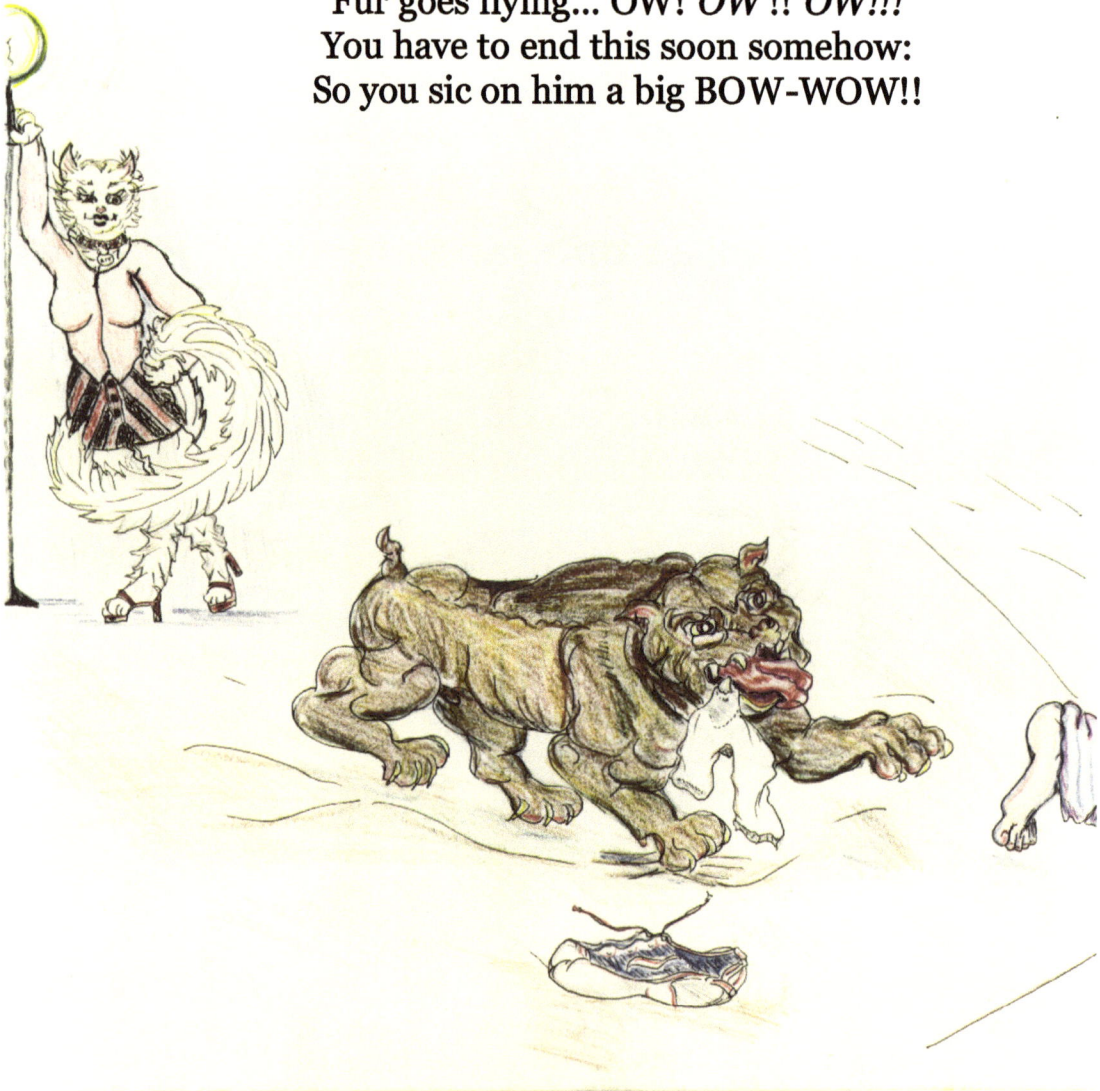

The Boys in Blue nicknamed him "The Barrel".
His job and abuse kept me in peril.
I'm grateful he slept with that girl Carol.
She gave him Syphilis, now he's sterile!

I hated his sly, *rotten* guts!
He drooled at <u>far</u> too many butts.
I just wanted to <u>crush his nuts</u>!!
He got *Death by the Thousand Cuts* !!!

All our years together and he couldn't give me a gold band. He deserved nothing less than going down s-l-o-w-l-y in QUICKSAND!

They say it always takes Two
Whether to quarrel or woo.
'Tho that is certainly true,
When One is caught in a coo,
The Other party is who
Is in a position to sue
For all that they can accrue
Because of that little screw!
Then it's just One in a stew--
One who is crying boo-hoo!!

When things got sappy,
He'd run for cover.
It'd make me happy
If he would hover.
He was just crappy
As a lover.
I went home snappy,
Back to Pappy.

IN BED AT NIGHT, I GOT ONLY REJECTION.
HIS TONE OF VOICE HELD A <u>NASTY</u> INFLECTION.
DAILY HE DEMANDED CONSTANT PERFECTION.
I ADMINISTERED A LETHAL INJECTION!

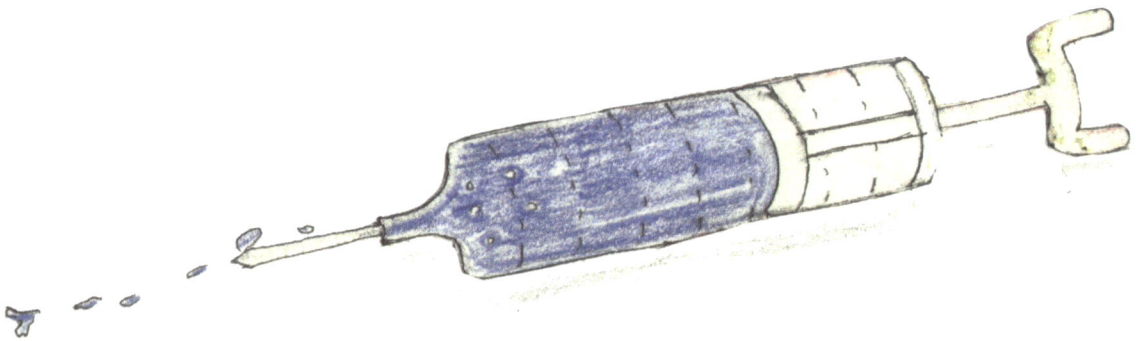

EACH TIME THAT HE WOULD CROON
A LOVELY LITTLE TUNE,
I SIMPLY WOULD JUST SWOON;
UNTIL, ONE DAY IN JUNE,
HE TURNED INTO A <u>GOON.</u>
I WISHED HIM TO THE MOON,
WHEN INTO THE SALOON
THERE SKITTERED A RACOON.
SHE WAS WILD -- 'TWAS A BOON!
HE WAS BIT AROUND NOON;
HE PASSED AWAY REAL SOON.

What can I say about my boyfriend Clark?
A man whose bite was as bad as his bark.
Many a time he left a nasty mark.
His demeanor was often cruel and dark.
I finally snapped and had a thought — Hark!
{Oh, what a whim! It would be such a *lark* !!}
He was KEELHAULED and EATEN by a shark!!!

HE SAID MY PRESENCE HAD BECOME AN IMPOSITION.
IT WAS TIME TO REVIVE THE SPANISH INQUISITION!!!

THEY REALLY THINK YOU'RE MADLY INSANE
WHEN YOU HOOK YOUR MAN ON TO A CRANE,
ATTACH HIM TO A WEATHER VANE,
AND WATCH HIM DROWN IN THUNDER AND RAIN.

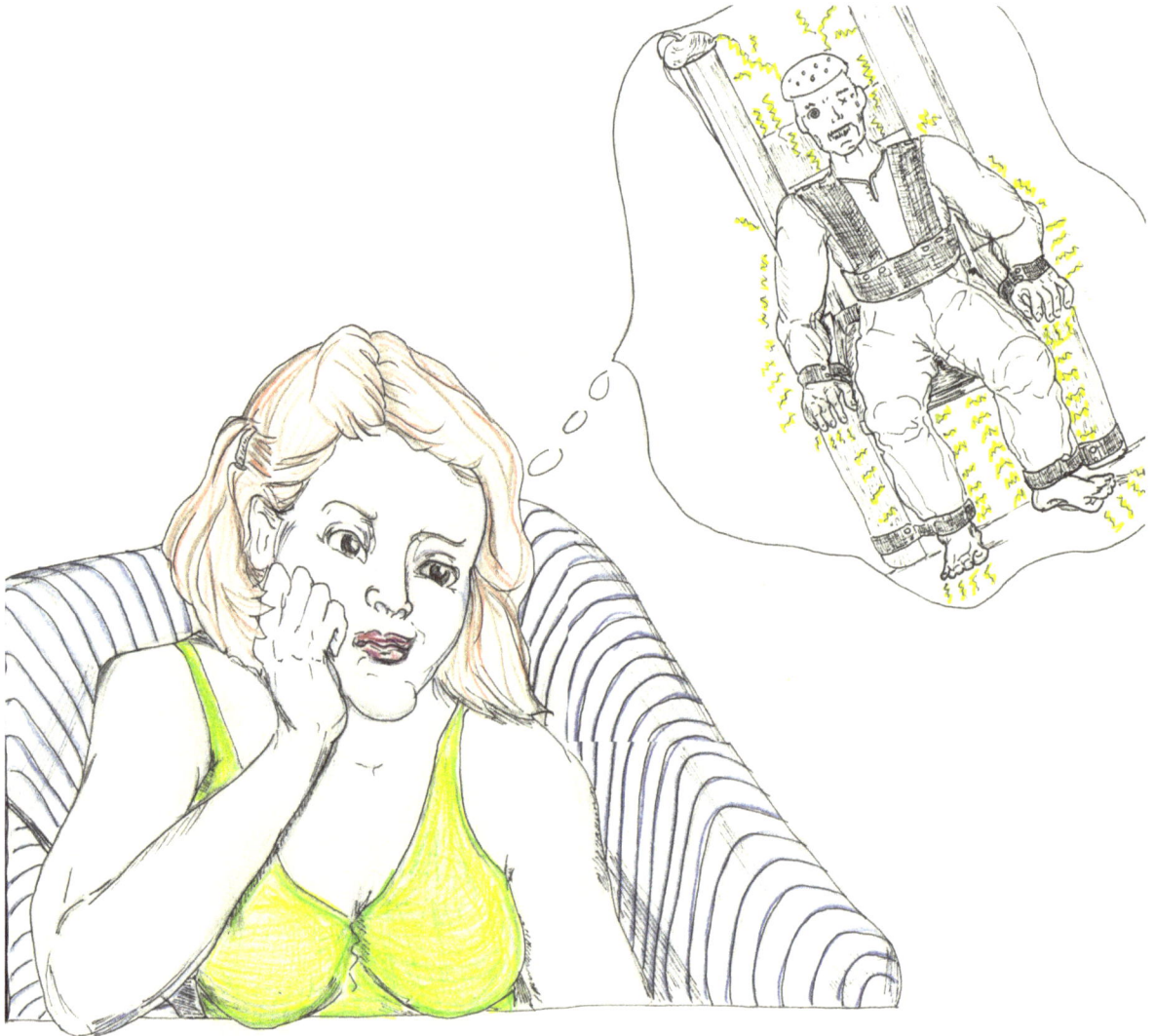

Over and over my darling Clyde lied,
So much so I could no longer abide.
He once stood staunchly by my side;
How he took my heart for quite a ride.
With remarks like how my hips were too wide,
My sensitive feelings and hurt couldn't hide.
Thus, for the sake of my womanly pride,
I couldn't keep letting all this stuff slide,
As night after night I cried and cried
And dreamt him in an electric chair, FRIED!
On the morrow, when my tears had dried,
Oh, how the sun doth turneth the tide!
Wonder just how my Clyde died?
I laced his drink with CYANIDE!!

When one is not really very nice,
Sometimes one pays a *terrible* price.
This poor chap, with his throw of the dice,
Gambled and lost -- with terms quite concise!
First, to be given a case of lice;
Lastly, toes to be eaten by mice.
For now, this much will have to suffice.

At naked bodies in Playboy he would peer.
"You never look this good," he'd say with a sneer.
Then later, possessively he'd grab my rear!
In disgust and scorn, I jabbed him with a SPEAR.

He said it was because I talked back;
He'd haul off and give me quite a whack.
After a time <u>anyone</u> would crack.
At his body I began to HACK.
I guess for this I had quite a knack,
'Cause he's deader than dead now, my Jack!

Oh that Wayne was exceedingly vain;
He'd stare at himself in a window pane...

It became such a great source of frustration;
The decree was death by DEFENESTRATION!!

"Don't do the crime if you can't do the time."
That's what they say when you don't get away.
I skated free on one *very* thin dime.
Because when I came down upon my prey,
I was as silent as a Mime!
Twas on a day when he was very gay,
But, to boot, an A-#1 prime slime!
My decision of death never did sway.
My method of choice was, oh, so sublime!
He was to gurgle his life's breath away
Struggling in a vat of LIME and grime.
I escaped here to San Francisco Bay
That's the story...the end of this rhyme.

Oh that Blake made my heart ache!
One day we drove out to the lake;
In the sand I placed a SNAKE.
<u>Never again</u> shall he take.

....

Now a new one's on the make.
"Hello gorgeous, my name's Drake."
I hope he's good...for his sake!

**Rick was such a dick
I hit him with a BRICK.**

Hot and heavy was our passion.
It began to pall after a fashion.
Seemed like sex was given in ration.
In love he was <u>not</u> my last bastion!

He made me act as if I were a *Nun*.
I reached in the dresser drawer for the GUN.
A single shot. Not merely just to stun.
No. For <u>weeks</u> I'd planned the deed to be done.

Happy now freedom is finally won,
I pull my hair down from its rigid bun,
Shouting, "You're no longer in control, son!
I'm goin' dancin' and have me some *fun* !!"

In his presence you just beam!
In his coffee you are the cream.
Of him at night you always dream,
As in your passion there's plenty of steam.
(Near always his eyes have a naughty gleam!)
He turns overnite a Cad and you deem
You must DRAW and QUARTER and hear him _scream_**!!**

{If for the feint of heart this is extreme,
Perhaps his character you can viciously REAM --
Or some other equally *dastardly* scheme!}

When first you meet, you're both in a daze.
Everything 'round you is in a haze.
Into his eyes you longingly gaze.
It's later that things become such a maze!
All your friends hope it's a passing phase.
You?--You want to set his home <u>ablaze</u>!!

SO THOROUGHLY DID HE ENJOY TRAVELIN'

WITH FLOOZIES WHOSE CLOTHES HE WAS UNRAVELIN',

HE SOARED FAR AT THE END OF MY JAVELIN!

Many moments with my Mitch
Were frankly quite a bitch;
Times *badly* had to switch.
A SPIN of the CAR WHEELS
Rolled him into a ditch!

If a little fun he would poke,
It was ok; I didn't care.
But *always* he made *me* the joke.
I thought, "Who's he? How does he dare?"
Never mind he was so broke!
(Yes, tit for tat, and fair is fair.)
Couldn't <u>even</u> afford a Coke!
Money disappeared into thin air.
I thought, "I've had it with this bloke."
When with lust at me he did stare,
Within was no fire to stoke;
Back at him I could only glare.
I dressed with dagger and a cloak
And waited on the spiral stair.
With his blood my BLADE I did soak!!
Then drug him to a far-off lair.
In my home next day I awoke
Glad, *GLAD*, GLAD he'd never be there!!!

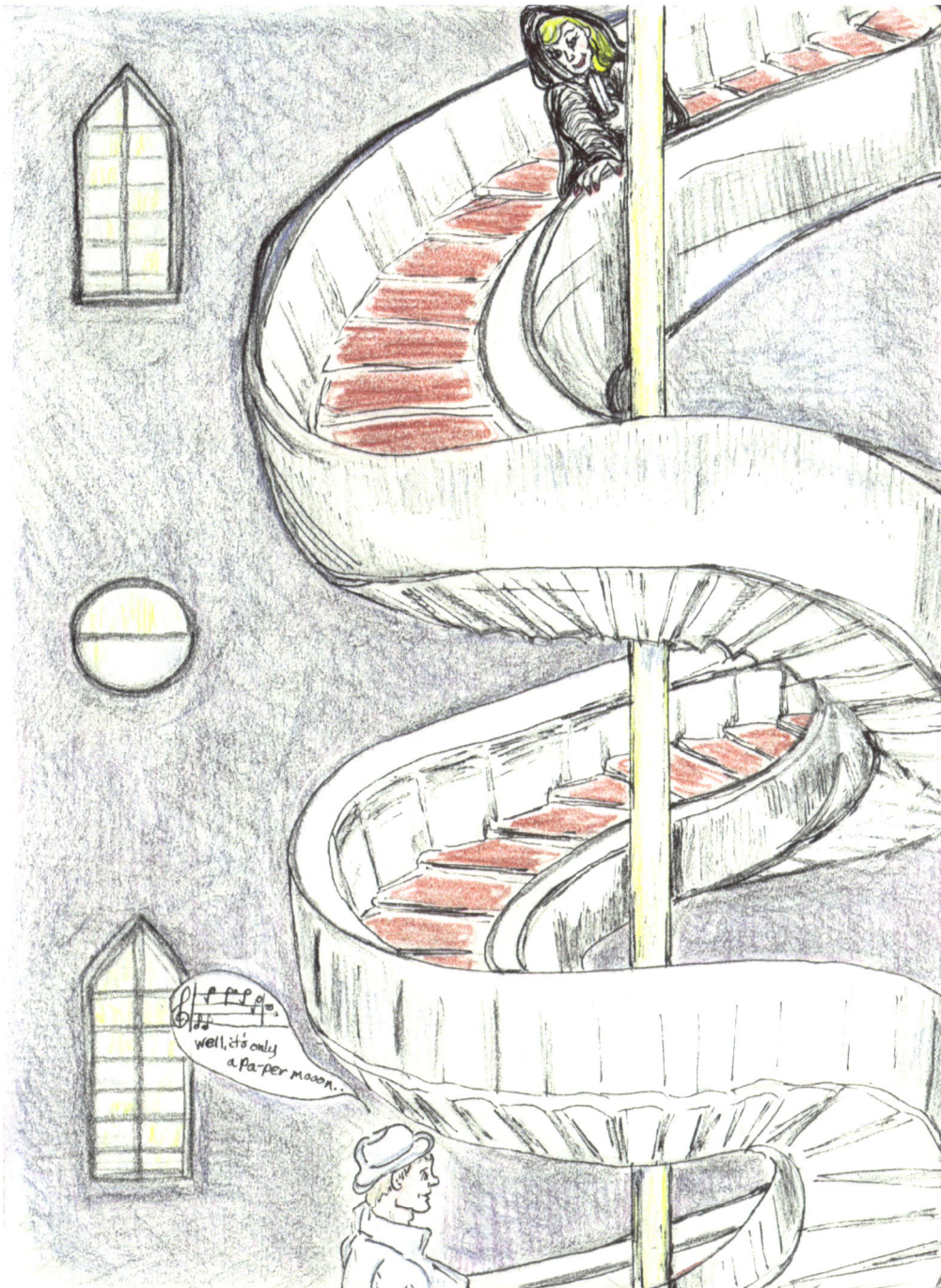

His disposition wasn't Sunny.
His humor wasn't very Funny.
I hated when he called me "Honey".
I absconded with all his Money.

This is a little tale of woe
Of a man who became my foe.
At first true love did smoothly flow;
All about us, the world did glow.
How he could make me melt, my Bo!
With his soft brown eyes like a doe,
And his good lovin'-- nice and slow.
Then EVIL surfaced, and *oh no* !
He was like something out of POE!
(—Worse than a bunion on a toe—)
When he pursued ho' after ho',
It was <u>far</u> too much of a blow.
They say "Ye shall reap what ye sow."
He got CASTRATION with a hoe.
{Thus endeth this tale of woe.}

"No, NO! I didn't. *Really!*" he cried.
I said, "I <u>saw</u> you, Brett. You just lied."
It was time he was trying to bide.
Too late--together they had been spied.
My last thread of patience had been tried.
So, up his body with ROPE I TIED;
SHRUNK his head, and on a SPIKE IT DRIED.

He'd tease, Tease, TEASE and slap, Slap, SLAP.
So I gave him the clap, Clap, CLAP!

Juan was such a *gorgeous* "fox",
With dark and thick flowing locks,
But treated me like dirty socks.
I injected him with the POX;
Now he's in a long pine box.

In the small town, the case caused quite a scandal.
It was the murder of a man named Randall.
Rumor says that to his girl he wasn't loyal;
That her clean reputation he did soil.
The poor thing couldn't take it; how she did snap.
Quick as a lick, she ended that boy's life—*WHAP* !
Incredibly, because he was such a dolt,
He didn't see it coming. . .the CROSSBOW Bolt.
Left on the scene was a lone sandal.
On no clues or proof could cops get a handle.
Without evidence, the case they had to close.
On the eve of his death, so the story goes,
Somewhere on a hill is lit a lone candle.

He was a dude with a passion for food.
Occasionally in the mood to brood.
In manners he could be quite crude.
At times comments and touch were lewd.

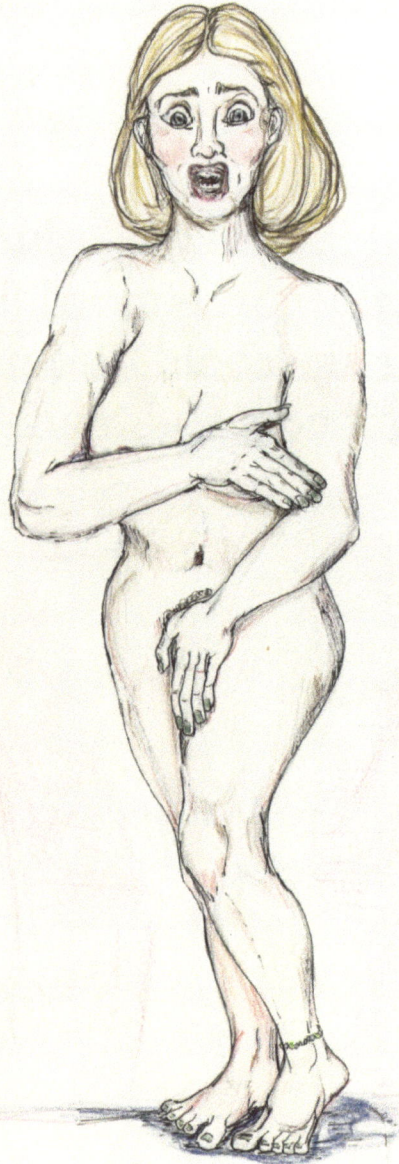

When in the nude, he thought me a prude.
{In that he was <u>exceedingly</u> rude!}

I simply *had* to have him STEWED.
That's what you get when you give me '*tude!!*

You killed our love, so now I'll kill you!
(Just as soon as I decide what to do.)
I'm sure it'll be a *gruesome* mess of goo!
Then I'll be free, and off with someone new.

He was always talking about his Id.
Bragging on end of great deeds he did.
In truth, I had to keep my bruises hid.
I hired a man with the lowest bid,
To BLOW his brains out the top of his lid.
I am joyous and free and of him rid!
Who did he think he bloody was, El Cid?

Kiss of Death Ditties

Hi. My name is Jane.
I live on Cain Lane.
Just because I've slain,
They think I'm not sane.

His name was Dwayne Dane.
He from my main vein
Did so slowly drain
The love I did gain.
MY SPIRIT DID WANE.

For Dwayne I did deign
To see him DEAD lain.

He died in no pain.
I cleaned up the stain,
Took a plane to Spain
To grow lots of grain--
And where I could reign
And living not feign.
WHERE YOU KNOW THAT RAIN,
IT STAYS ON THE PLAIN.

Tsk.
(Shoulda been a train
Down to the Ukraine.)

Hi. My name is Jane.
They think I'm insane....

His need for attention made me weary;
Of his rotten temper I was leery.
Life began to be so drab and dreary.
'Tho this may seem quite a bit *eerie*,
When next he got stinkin' drunk and bleary
I *INCINERATED* him, dearie!
(I'm pleased as punch and not a bit teary!)

When his moods were sunny,
Life was bright and funny.
When all was cloudy and grey,
There was big-time hell to pay.
When push came to shove,
It was time to end this abusive love.
We took a trip to the White Cliffs of Dover,
Where I very quickly HEAVED HIM OVER!

As a farmer, he never had a good crop.
As a lover, he was just an utter flop!
What to do? Dump him, and go out with a cop.

Even games with him were a bore.
He found sex to be quite a chore--
Signs enough *all* to declare war!
But when I found him with a whore
(And not just one: there were *FOUR* !)
He'd hit me at my very core.
Should I just kick him out the door?
NO! It had to be SO much more.
Yes! An Iron Maiden! What for?
A cool way to produce much GORE!
And *lots* and *lots* of BLOOD to *POUR* !
As through his flesh the blades they tore,
Stuff did spurt out of every pore!
In TERRIBLE pain he did roar,
And from my heart a song did soar.
He'll not be cheating *ANYMORE!*

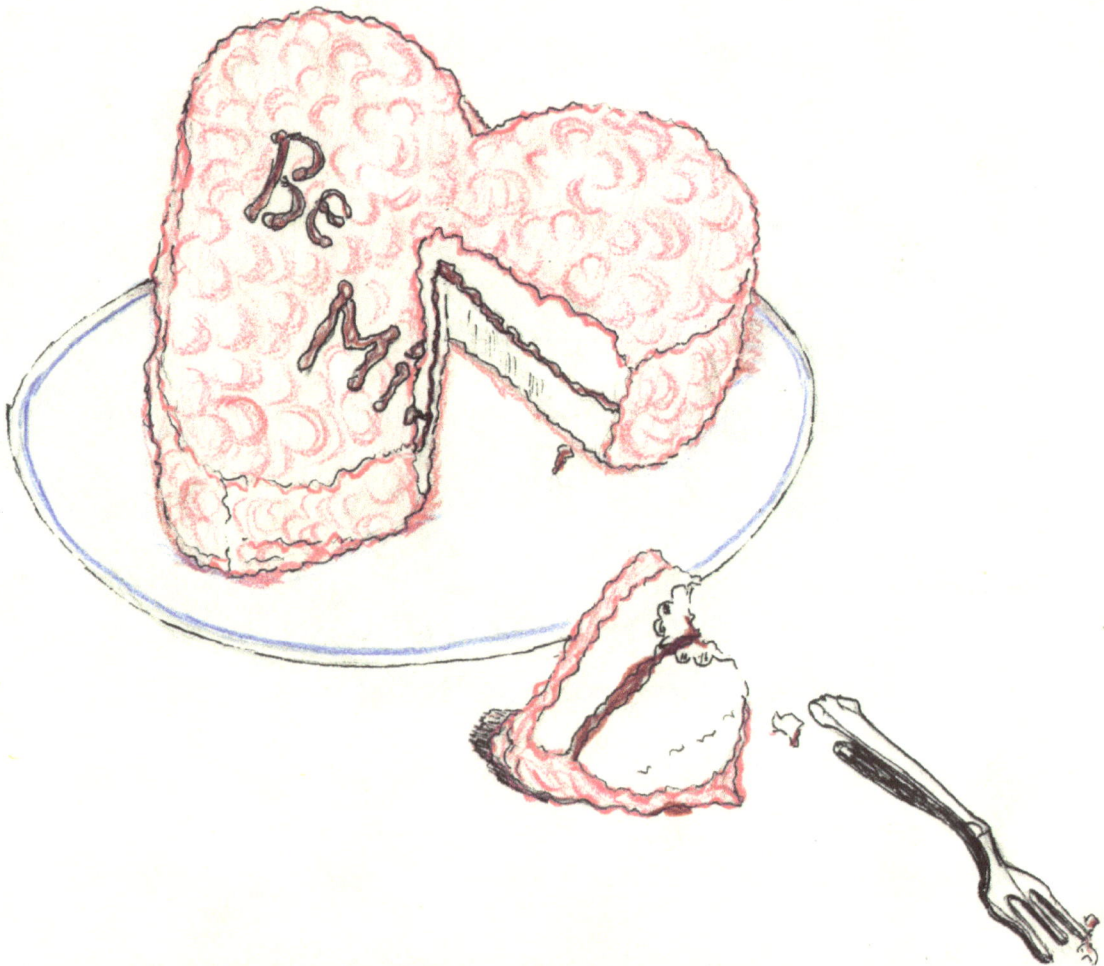

Jake was such a rake,
A big fat phoney fake.
Said I was a flake;
Oh my heart he did break!
But do not forsake;
For Jake I did bake
A POISONous cake--
Then I went to his wake!

"Baby, ya gotta go on a diet.
Come on," he'd coax her, "Try it, you'll like it."
But Weight Watchers--she just couldn't buy it.
Told him his new home could be the Hyatt!
Now finally she has peace and quiet.

HE HURT ME DEEP WHEN HONESTY HE DID LACK,
THUS I STABBED HIM once, Twice, THRICE--IN THE BACK!!!

I was always Green with jealousy
of attention to other women he gave.
But now that I've stabbed him
THREE TIMES IN THE HEART --
He'll give nothing to no-one!
(The poor, poor knave.)

Our life together was pure *heaven*.
We had the <u>whole pie</u>, not just a slice.
Though our years as one numbered seven,
Seemed just yesterday was thrown the rice.

Then one day his love turned straight to stone!
The beauty of our union was blown.
I could have with grace bid him adieu,
Even perhaps remaining friends too.

Instead, his death made the front-page news,
And I took an around-the-world cruise!

When first she saw him, she just <u>flipped</u>!
Later, she began to feel gypped.
It seemed as if he spoke from script;
In that way his hand he tipped.
So first he was *thoroughly* WHIPPED;
Secondly, in mummy-cloth DIPPED;
Last, he was thrown into a CRYPT!

He always acted like a dope:
Mostly he'd sit around and mope.
When he did move, he'd slowly lope.
Of his life's plan he had no scope.
She quite simply just couldn't cope.
Of a break she could only hope.
Aha! She dressed him all in Taupe,
And HUNG him with a matching rope!

At first Carl was very kind and good;
He even lived in the neighborhood.
When he didn't treat her as he should,
They took a little walk to a wood.
There she SHOT him where he stood.

During the day he's been <u>insulting</u> and a *grump*!
Bedtime comes; he cajoles 'cause he wants to hump.
Suggest he's a baseball player; you play Ump;
Three strikes, he-e-e-e 's <u>OUT!!!</u> Tonite he gets no grind or bump!

For wrongful neglect he was to blame
He always had to *ask* if I came!
His arousal techniques were quite lame.
He was forced to wear The MASK of SHAME.

His womanizing threw me into such a **rage**,
At the Zoo I pushed him into the Lion's cage.
Where I noticed with <u>glee</u> in the corner he cowered,
And I watched as he was *voraciously* DEVOURED.

He was a gent with a sexy drawl.
I *thrilled* with every late-nite call.
How he could swing me 'round the dance hall.
When my body he began to maul,
What <u>nerve</u>! What unmitigated *gall!*
I CHOPPED him up without further stall,
And BRICKED him up inside the wall.

Jim was full of vigor and vim,
Kept his physique slim and trim.
But ofttimes he was pretty dim--
Sometimes mighty neat and prim.
Wanted to tear him limb from limb!
Instead I decided, on a whim,
That he should meet my good friend Tim.
Now they're quite a pair: Tim and Jim!

"All right, All right!" cried the Lady Bess.
"In my heart I know I must confess,
So that the Lord my soul will bless.
It started when he took a Mistress.
I'm his betrothed, and not yet Countess!
Gossip of his dalliance is, I guess,
What caused my mind to be in distress.
When next he drank spirit in excess,
His head I had CRUSHED in the Duck Press.
As his brains splattered onto my dress,
The servants rushed to clean up the mess.
That's all I remember, more or less.
I loved him, you see," lamented Bess.

**BECAUSE TO ME HE WAS ALWAYS MENACING,
THE PUNISHMENT FOR THIS CRIME WAS NECKLACING.**

When a man has you in his spell And
he's tearing your heart asunder, How
do you get <u>out</u> of that *HELL* ?
BURY HIM ALIVE , six feet under!!

Dane was really quite inane.
Never, *ever* used his brain.
His existence was my bane.
So I CRACKED him with a CANE.

Time spent with Paul was always a ball!
(Especially shopping at the mall).
When he began to constantly brawl,
I made him to our window sill crawl
In our building that was, oh, so tall.
He died from a twenty-story FALL.

I could no longer put up a pretense.
Let's face it--my beau was pretty darn dense.
He was as thick as the post of a fence!
Hence, I had to do what made the most sense:
Dress him pretty and sell him for SIX-PENCE!!

BEAU*
reduced!
only 6¢

It wasn't that he had feet of clay.
It was all those women, day after day,
Who he'd lay in stack of hay after hay.
(Not even in the merry month of May!)
Gosh, I thought, what will people say?
There's a lesson here, but who was to pay?
I decided *he* should, and *I* would slay.
He begged for mercy and began to pray,
As with my Ginsu I commenced to FLAY.
Never more will another heart he play.

He was a <u>swine</u>! I made him a cuckold!
And like those poor accused witches of old,
I ordered him to ride the ducking stool.
Pity he to be such a fool.

He was Mean, Nasty, Cruel, and Low.
She shouted "Off to Archery class I go!"
There she learned to master her trusty bow
Practiced pulling the arrow to and fro,
Patiently waiting for her skills to grow.

At last she was ready. Ha, Ha! Ho, Ho!
When next he was in her sights just so,
She aimed for her target and struck a blow!
Now that No-Good-Man is no mo'!!

He was one of those "I Rule The Roost" types of men. You know...the kind who order you about where and when. He then wanted me to be a Mother Hen of <u>TEN</u>!!
So I wrote a "Dear John" letter to Ben with my pen--
Said I was flying the coop to build a nest with Glen!!!

They bring you flowers and candy and such,
Tell you they love you oh so much,
Treat you like crystal in a hutch --
Then one day tell you they hate you a bunch!
Your little heart in pain you clutch,
For you became nothing more than a crutch.
He tells you at dinner; and as you munch,
Plot to give him ARSENIC next day at Brunch!
You do--and now he's dead cold to the touch.

You stick with them through thick and thin,
Cry when another they strive to win;
What else to do but ponder . . . and *grin*
When at last you plot to do them in!

With me he always played fast and loose.
Now he swings a new way--from a NOOSE!

He said, "You're looking quite like a frump.
No longer are you just pleasingly plump.
My God, girl! Look at the *size* of your <u>rump</u>!"
I CHOPPED him up till he was just a stump,
Bagged him, and threw him in the garbage dump.

He was full of so much jive
She took him for a SKY-DIVE.
Alas, poor man, he's <u>not</u> *Alive!*

You weep and weep because he is gone.
Do you think he's out crying in his beer?
Will you forever after him want to fawn
While he's out giving the next chick a leer?
How do you erase him and move on?
After all, he's giving a *huge* cheer!
When, oh when, will reason ever dawn?

When, oh *when*, will it ever be clear?
Perhaps you would feel less of a pawn
If you found something about which to jeer.
Hell no! Date someone of really big brawn
Who could SPILL HIS GUTS all over the lawn!
Then you'll jump for joy and shed not one tear;
You'll gleefully say "Bozo, you're *OUTTA HERE!*"

Most times he was quite gentle, my Wes.
So polite, every word a caress;
Always helping me on with my shawl.
Suddenly, he would turn quite *monstrous* —
Literally something out of Loch Ness!
One time I was under <u>such</u> duress
That I poked his eyes out with an AWL!
Without sight he's utterly helpless.
Frankly, my dear, I couldn't care *less!*

She said, "LOOK HERE! THIS IS THE HUNT, HON'!
AT THE START OF THE SET OF THE SUN,
YOU ARE TO GET YOUR BUTT ON THE RUN!
'THO THIS BUCKSHOT RIFLE WEIGHS A TON,
I'LL KILL YOU. BUT YOU'RE JUST NUMBER *ONE*!
THEN <u>ALL</u> MEN LIKE YOU TILL THERE ARE NONE!!"
She did. Now those types number 'UN'.

All he ever said was "You won't." and "You can't."
Never "Sure honey, go right on ahead."
Into VOODOO I delved and began to chant;
Six months later (*kiss that doll!*) he was dead!

He didn't exactly sing like Bing;
But with each note, my heart it did cling.
He then did bring me under his wing;
And, oh, how my heart it did zing!
Next did happen a *horrible* thing.
Like a slap with a long-lasting sting,
Guitar Man wouldn't give me a ring!!
I GARROTTED him with his "G" string!!!

He was a filthy bum.
A low-down dirty scum.

Did I mention how *dumb* ?

Never lifted a thumb
In picking up <u>one</u> crumb.
Our home looked like a slum.

He brought us not a sum.
As it all went to Rum.

(How nourishing: yum, yum.)

I began to feel glum.
Our life was so hum-drum.

He'd sit around and hum
Songs about dear old Mum
Till my mind plumb went numb!

Certain demise, by gum,
Was inspiration from
<u>THE PIT AND THE PENDULUM</u>!!

When working out wasn't enough of a pump,
He'd grasp my hair in his fist in one big clump,
Hurl me into walls till my face was a lump.
I suggested he'd enjoy a BUNGEE jump.
Tragically, he hit his head with quite a thump!

Because his behavior was so foul,
There was <u>extreme</u> need to DISEM*BOWEL*.

He was such a <u>pitiful</u> Knave,
Could seemingly never behave.
'Tho of his *prowess* I could rave,
He was <u>not</u> the dutiful slave.
Thus, to the priest I amply gave
Money to mark the place of his grave.

Of his talents I was always awed,
But hated when he called me a "broad".
Instead of caressing, he just pawed.
In all his actions, he proved a fraud.
Right IN HALF I had him SAWED.

His only goal was to get me abed.
So I BLUDGEONED him with a pipe of lead.
Then fled with his large hidden stash of bread,
Booking myself a long trip to Club Med!

I slowly began to dread
Each time I had to see Ted.
After I was flattered and fed,
He'd play mind-games with my head--
Then wish to kiss and go to bed!
After a while, I saw red,
Kept wishing he was, oh, *SO* dead.
'Tho he said he wanted to wed,
Instead I PUMPED him FULL OF LEAD,
And off I fled with Ed and Fred!!

He treated me as if I were a leper.
I knew he was allergic to red pepper;
I sprinkled some in the dish I was cooking
(And had to forget he was so good-looking).
As he ate, I watched as he struggled to breathe,
Remembering what to me he would bequeath!
I didn't lift a finger to help, you see--
Just waited for the end and calmly drank tea.

**WHAT TO DO WHEN HE'S THE BIGGEST JERK IN THE NATION?
WHY *DAHLING* , COMMIT CHARACTER ASSASSINATION!**

His personality was quite placid,
During sex he was frequently flaccid.
I pumped his veins full of PRUSSIC ACID!

Ah, Pierre had such a cute derriere.
But I had a problem with his little butt:

It found its way to slut after slut!
So now when people ask
Where, oh where, oh *where* is Pierre?,
I simply say:

"I shut him up, in a little hut;
and now he's quite, *quite* off his nut!"

Joe thought he was, oh, so cool--
When really he was too, *too* cruel.
Tried to buy me with <u>fur and jewel</u>!
I don't generally, as a rule,
Fall for men who think me a fool.
I'd rather DROWN them in a pool
After SMITING them with a blunt tool!

Bill was such a dill of a pill.
Of his women I'd had my fill.
<u>Very</u> strong was my will to kill.
Into him I wanted to drill
Bullets until his breathing was nil.
But 'twas his rendezvous with Jill
That broke the last straw of my will.
There atop the grassy hill,
They kissed and wrote love poems--till
I punctured their carotids with the QUILL !

SEAN WAS TALL, AND BY TRADE WAS A PRINTER.
HE FORCED ME TO READ (YUCK!) HAROLD PINTER!
IN MY BUTT HE BECAME A BIG SPLINTER--
THERE WAS A SKIING MISHAP IN WINTER!!

He said he'd keep her safe from harm;
It was all just part of the charm.
So let's just say -- he bought the farm!

He was very *sneaky*.
He had to be stopped.
This may seem *freaky*,
But off his head I LOPPED.
When it hit the floor,
It kind of Ker-plopped.
I flew out the door —
To a dinner date I hopped!

I used to *adore* Morty.
Never treated me like dirt
Till the year he turned forty--
Chasing every little skirt.
Then he got fat and warty.
Bottom line? So long, Shorty!

He always wore a very sharp hat.
Turns out he was a Dirty Rat.
She hit him with a baseball bat,
Screaming "Take that! and that!! *and that* !!!
and that!!!! "

**FOR HIM I WAS FILLED WITH *HATE!, HATE!!, <u>HATE</u>!!!*
I DECIDED TO *D E C A P I T A T E !!!!*

How and why did it come to this --
His wanting a new pretty, young Miss?
I kept my figure and colored my hair.
It's only my age . . . It just isn't fair!
Doesn't he see it's because of his Bucks?!
She's got the car; now *that* really <u>SUCKS</u>!
She'll tool around town spending his money,
And coddle and coo and call him "honey",
Wrapping him around her finger until...

He won't even see her come in for the KILL!!
I wonder if I should save him or not,
When for me he no longer cares a jot.
Or should I on both commit foul play?
NO, NO! . . . It's better that day by day
I watch *him* grow old and grey,
And wrinkled and wizened, his brain but a prune.
She'll make him sign papers that mark him a Loon!

As he's carted off, he'll think life's a bitch --
As we girls link hands and become RICH, *RICH*, *RICH!!!*